vitamins

of

hope

volume two

pamela fields

S.H.E. PUBLISHING, LLC

Vitamins of Hope | Volume Two
Copyright © 2021 by Pamela Fields.

All rights reserved. Printed in the United States of America. No part of this book may be used or reproduced in any manner whatsoever without written permission except in the case of brief quotations embodied in critical articles or reviews.

For information contact :
info@shepublishingllc.com
www.shepublishingllc.com

Book Cover and Title Page design by Michelle Phillips of
CHELLD3 3D VISUALIZATION AND DESIGN

ISBN :
9781953163349 (paperback)

First Edition : November 2021

10 9 8 7 6 5 4 3 2 1

CONTENTS

1 | A FORGOTTEN COMMODITY

2 | WORDS OF FLAVOR

3 | INTRICATE WEBS OF LIFE

4 | IT SHALL COME TO PASS

5 | HEARTFELT PRAYERS OF A MOTHER

6 | KNOCK, KNOCK, KNOCKING AT THE DOOR

7 | ESCALATING SIN

8 | DEAR DAUGHTER:

9 | TWENTY-ONE YEARS

10 | IN THE CLOSET OF MY MIND

11 | THE MAN BEHING THE ANOINTING

12 | DEATH ROW REQUEST

13 | A SPIRITUAL TUNE UP

14 | WANTED, A SOLDIER

15 | THE LOVE OF GOD

16 | SQUEEZE IT OUT

17 | THE BREATH OF LIFE

18 | CROSSROADS OF LIFE

19 | A DIFFERENT KIND OF TREE

20	RENEWED WINGS
21	AN IMPORTANT MAN
22	MENDING BURDENS
23	QUICKSAND
24	SCATTER THE SEEDS
25	IN THE NAME OF JESUS...
	INTERMISSION
26	SUCCESSFUL...
27	HAVE YOU EVER...
28	THE ENLIST
29	FAITH IN THE BAG
30	BUILDING A SOUL
31	A POOL OF TEARS
32	THE CHARACTER OF THE ROSE
33	AT THE GRAVESITE
34	AMALIKITES
35	COBWEBS
36	THE SPIRITUAL RODEO
37	THAT'S JOY
38	THE WRONG ROOM

39 | DRINKING THE FLUIDS OF LOVE

40 | UNUTTERED COMMUNICATION

41 | COMING IN FROM THE STORM

42 | WHERE IS THE GOOD TEACHERS' GRAVEYARD?

43 | SLAVE

44 | SPICES

45 | THE BLIND MAN

46 | SPIRIT OF STRUGGLE

47 | THAT UNEXPLAINABLE FEELING

48 | ANGELS AT THE DOOR

49 | A LAWYER IN THE COURTROOM

50 | THE PROCEDURE

ACKNOWLEDGMENTS

ABOUT THE AUTHOR

vitamins

of

hope

volume two

pamela fields

1 | A FORGOTTEN COMMODITY

The world is processed,
And there is an instant remedy
To any given situation in life.

The mind is a powerful tool
And the heart is responsive to the compassion
Which acts as a motivating factor.

Like computers, the programs
To our life is already written
In a book called LAWS.

There is yet a Higher Element in life,
A Power that's divine. The LAWS
And principals in this book, we choose not.

Neatly and cleverly disguised
Beneath the beauty that airs
Within the modern and sophisticated cities of the world.

Greed and a struggle for power
An open display of backbiting and lust,
TV and news reporters uncover the shame in every era.

And this is the crime we teach our children
A forgotten commodity of treasures

PAMELA FIELDS

More precious than gold, minds just waiting to be
Discovered, covered mines a prospector's joy.

The mind of man has explored the technologies
Of the Earth, but how will they unlock the
Purest form of a commodity being wasted.

How will they redevelop the wastelands and
Rebuild its promises of dreams long broken when
The minds of our youth have lost sight of them?

Our perverse actions and our inconsistencies makes
A statement, a very hurtful statement when this
A proven harmful era neglects its wealth.

Young minds are deprived the chance
To express and to be heard. They are
Deprived the chance to love and to be loved.

It deprives them of the opportunity to grow because
It chisels bits and pieces of this perfect mold the
Pick of injustice still found in the one hand with the
Other, the shovel of the LAW removes the evidence.

A perfect world of law and order
When it submits to the heart
As seen in the purest form of mankind.

And when love is evicted, the door remains open to
Allow a corrupt system to penetrate the membranes
And to smother and suck out any residues of what
Once lived there.

VITAMINS OF HOPE

The idea of love, processed in the mind
Through the world systems. Instance remedies
Of what is suppose to happen slips in place.

Using the world's lust and greed,
Backbiting, lying, killing and stealing becoming the
Masters of Ceremony.

And it teaches an already bent heart, that it's crooked.

How to claw its way in society
The programs already etched.

A drilling effect, processed and ready.
Instance results, but at what price?

But when we refine the nuggets of a child's mind
Measured by the pureness of the carats of his heart,
Earth's technology and the divine LAW of God
interchangeably.

A mine, like a bomb igniting
Exploding when the prospectors' techniques
Have learned to wash away the by-products
Of a sinful nature when exploring the tunnels of the
mind.

2 | WORDS OF FLAVOR

An appetizing speech

    Appealing in all that

        You have to say.

All the right words

    Bring colors bursting

        With flavor.

Oranges and limes

    Cherry and peach

        Oh my, what a speech.

3 | INTRICATE WEBS OF LIFE

How careless we weave
  The intricate webs of our own life.

Turns upon turns upon loops
  Tightly sprung into knots.

Untying the knots
  In a desperate effort to straighten the mess.

Knots, representative of
  Problems and obstacles that leave us nowhere.

A maze, dark and lonely
  As we try to unravel the intricate mess.

Tangled up and cleverly scattered
  Endless spans of life's journeys.

Take my hand Dear Jesus,
  And take me safely till I reach the end.

The web's we weave ourselves in life
  Are tangled webs when carelessly we weave.

4 | IT SHALL COME TO PASS

My spirit is dancing
And waving banners in the air.

The joyous feelings
Rushes through my soul.

As I run in my excitement
I am very conscience
That I am about to board
A most prestigious train.

But my spirit is received
And welcomed by
One most Powerful.

Oh, how many times past
I've missed, never even knowing
That this train even existed.

It all started with the contract meeting.
Those in attendance in the conference room
Were very humble, they knew that
This was a Divine Appointment.

VITAMINS OF HOPE

I was there and now
My soul rejoice mightily.

Oh what a joy it is
To be aboard this train of Life.

For you see, at the board meeting
I was given the key to open up
The door to wealth and success.

A much needed token
For advancement
On this train of Life.

But wait, I must hurry
To catch this train
It has it's boarding signals on.

If I had not caught it
Life was preparing to
Bury me alive because of my lack.

I'm walking in the surety of my calling
A little more each day.

But today, I think I'll ride
The sweet train of Life.

5 | HEARTFELT PRAYERS OF A MOTHER

My job, I thank you for giving me the strength
    To make each and every day,
        And for helping me completing the week.

My son, cover his head with the blood of Jesus.
    Open up his eyes concerning the word and plan
        According to your will for his life.

My youngest, give her to know that I love her Lord.
    But most of all, give her to know and to feel
        Your love for her. Bless her Father.

My oldest, it is my prayer that you convict her even now.
    Give her how to be a good parent.
        Lord, help her to focus toward her future.
            Rebuke the devil and that hindering spirit.

Lord, as their mother, teach me, show me how to
    Love and strengthen me where I'm weak.
        Show me Dear Lord, to be an effective mother.
            Rebuke anything in me that is not like you.
        Take it away, Lord.

VITAMINS OF HOPE

Please Lord, never stop talking to my heart.

My husband, I can't continue to hold up in prayer,
    Although he is most needful. Please kind Sir,
        Share with me your perfect will.

Your servant is deliriously exhausted, trying very
    Hard not to complain. For all of my efforts am
        I bruised, sore and battered in the spirit.

Help me Father, to get my household in order.
    And in line with your will for our lives.

Souls on every turn, Lord
    Teach me how to war in the spirit and out.
        Forgive me this day.

                Amen

6 | KNOCK, KNOCK, KNOCKING AT MY DOOR

Jesus turned on the light of my soul one day
    When He raised the shades of my spirit.

I opened up the door of my heart
    And aired it out.

He swept away the dust.
    Then washed me, scrubbed me
        Until I was clean.

Rung me out
    Rinsed and rung me out again.

Now He's polishing
    And shining me up good.

So that His reflection
    He'll be able to see.

And that others will see
    His reflection in me.

7 | ESCALATING SIN

Oh the many things that the devil will say to us
Using the mind, will he tell you:

> I wonder how it would be just to try it...
>
> I'll get saved next week...
>
> I'm stronger than the others...
>
> I can kick this habit anytime...
>
> It can't happen to me...
>
> I'm still young...
>
> I want to have fun...

Escalating sin
> In a perverse and wicked world.

The Bible says
> That the heart is deceitfully wicked.
>
> Yet says the mind, "God knows my heart."

Perverse, because
> The mind of man is not disciplined to the will of God.

PAMELA FIELDS

He knows the will of God, but this he do not.
    The thing that he should not do, this he do.

The things that the mind will tell you
    Because the tree of wickedness stems from the
    Seed of sin and grows in the heart of man.

Thus, sin has become
    A passion
    A past time
    A hobby

And the heart of man lust for it,
    It feels good to man.

8 | DEAR DAUGHTER:

You're stuck dwelling over the itty-bitty struggles of life, when your focus should be on achieving outstanding benefits and rewards.

Your special trail is a screen, a camouflage, neatly disguising what is tucked away behind door number one. However, door number two has its unique prize. And door number three is totally a disaster.

You know, sometimes we do that to our own lives, make a total and complete disaster of it. While other times we settle for second best. When the grand prize is what we want.

The point is, our actions today determine our gifts and rewards of tomorrow.

In life's clutter of problems, each coming one behind the other, it's so easy to loose one's focus and miss the opportunity to score. Like a fast ball and even the curve balls of life, as it approaches, that ball so easily is swung at and missed unless our focus is sure.

Problems are the ground work that adults walk. Problems pave the course and the crossroads are the many decisions in which we encounter daily.

Understanding that there is always an option, like true and false questions, or the multiple choice of a school exam.

PAMELA FIELDS

Even essay quizzes, through seldom required, may ask your opinion. But in life's big monopoly, opinions really don't matter. Until the one day you become head of the firm
or a leader amongst people.

This is, after all, the true focus to aim for.

Lovingly,

Your Mother,
And Friend

9 | TWENTY-ONE YEARS

Twenty-one years, I've prepared you for this day.

I know I'm forgetting something that I need to tell you, so just always remember as you pave your road through life:

>The most important unit, is the family.

>So call whenever you need anything.

>Visit often.

Don't stray too far from the things I've tried to teach you.

>Eat right.

>Stay in school.

>Go to church.

>Smiling make you feel better.

>Brush your teeth every day and night.

>Give yourself time to dry off after a shower in cold weather.

PAMELA FIELDS

My how the time past. Here today and tomorrow, it's just a blur.

>Be good to yourself.

>Don't drink.

>Don't use drugs.

>Don't smoke.

>Protected sex is still not safe sex,
>it's a sin when you're not married.

>Avoid credit.

>A husband findeth a wife,
>and not the other way around.

>Believe in God.

>Faith is a good thing.

Oh my, how the time surely pass.

>So use time wisely.

>Finish projects.

>Respect deadlines.

>Pay your bills on time.

>Gambling is not faith.

>Respect authority.

>Pray over important decisions.

VITAMINS OF HOPE

Doctors don't know everything, get a second opinion.

Threats should be limited to things you can carry through.

And if you're ever so blessed to become prosperous ...
Remember!

> Remember the church,
> and give them a tenth of your earnings.
>
> You can gain the whole world but
> what would it profit you to lose your soul?
>
> It's easier to find a needle in a haystack then for a rich
> man to enter into the kingdom of heaven.

This is important so pay very close attention:

> Life can be very difficult if you are void understanding.
> So, in all thy getting, get understanding.
>
> Rules and regulations are a part of life,
> everybody has to follow them.
>
> Man made rules, called laws,
> like stopping at the red light.
>
> And the laws of the heart, which is what God looks at,
> called commandments, Love your neighbor as yourself.

10 | IN THE CLOSET OF MY MIND

In the closet of my mind
In the very clutches of my mind
Spark's hope.

In the darkest day
Rays of fire direct my way.

In the blackest night
A twinkle of joy guides my plight.

When I close my eyes
The light of my soul in prayer lies.

In the deepest valley
Shines faith from the highest mountain.

When all is lost
The dawning of a new day, like pearls of life cost.

When death and destruction surround you
Try Jesus, He is the way out.

11 | THE MAN BEHIND THE ANOINTING

He's appointed and anointed to serve almighty God.

He's committed by the vows to serve in whatever way he can.

He's led by the spirit as to which way to go.

He prays for the sick. He teaches and preaches to all mankind.

It seems that the spirit is satisfied, but the man it left behind.

He asked God for help to help him run this race.

It seems that it never comes, but he continues to obey.

But one day as that man lay sleeping,
God comes to please the man.

He takes away a rib, and then He creates woman.

She listens to him when he cries, and wipe his tears away.

Then man decided to make woman his wife.

PAMELA FIELDS

But it can never be complete without God in both their lives.

So they must always remember who gave them to each other.

And thank God every day.

Then they will always walk together and never go astray.

He is no longer just an anointed and appointed man of God.

He's become a husband, a friend and a lover.

And a mighty man of God!

By Angelina Cooks

12 | DEATH ROW REQUEST

The day has finally come and there is one request, the warden has said, "You can have anything you want to eat. You can call anyone you want to call. You can choose your way of death, lethal injection, electrocution, or gas chamber."

He chose to eat the word of God. If any man die though he be dead, yet shall he live again. He chose to call 1-800-Jesus. He asked God for forgiveness. He accepted Jesus into his heart. He confessed and believed that He died and rose again.

He took a stand, that if he died, his choice would be to die in Christ. Even if he's not put to death, he would not walk around spiritually dead.

He requested God to spare his life. Forgiveness, the mother of the man he had killed. The call to the governor by the mother.

The pardon came at 12:01.

By Angelina Cooks

13 | A SPIRITUAL TUNE UP

It starts in your heart; the distressful soul starts getting tired.
It seems if through you're falling apart, no matter what you do.
There is no peace, your joy is gone. It seems that you're all alone.

It seems your oil is running low. There is no fuel getting to the engine of your soul. It seems that you're missing something. Your life just doesn't seem complete.

Some days you can get started. Some days you won't start at all.
Then out of nowhere, there is a call and your heart gets thirsty.
For a spiritual refill.

You pull into the secret place for a spiritual tune up.
Looking for God to show up to change your spiritual spark,
Your thoughts.

To flush out your carburetor, there is no oil coming.
To put air into the tires of your soul. It seems as though your
Wind shield wiper can't wipe your tears away.

VITAMINS OF HOPE

It seems as though your
heart gets heavier with every word you say.
It seems as if God is not listening to a word that you pray.
You're thankful that you've made it this far,
and God never let you down.

You're wondering by this time, will He just let you down?
Then the negative connects with the positive, and it feels like
electric shock. Suddenly you feel your strength being renewed.
Then you'll know that God is listening, because
you start looking alive again.

By Angelina Cooks

14 | WANTED, A SOLDIER

As I go through the gutter, lost souls are all I see. It saddens me.

Tell me Lord, what to do?

Sometimes it's a sister, and sometimes it's a brother. Death is all around me.

They are falling by the way side,
being wash down the sewer.

Jesus picked fishermen, now he is picking street cleaners to labor for the harvest, for the lost souls.

We must check every alley, every crack and dope house, every liquor store, every homeless shelter. There are so many places to look. They're everywhere, in the hospitals. Wailing for the answer. When the doctors

VITAMINS OF HOPE

Have given up, and even in the jail house, with steel bracelets on their hands and feet.

Just waiting for some strong God-fearing soldier to tell them, Jesus can make them free.

Wanted: Soldiers for the army of the Lord.

By Angelina Cooks

15 | THE LOVE OF GOD

Many times, God has put us in a ministry for a season. Ecc. 3 But when the season comes and it is time for change, we don't want to let go. We don't want to see others leave. Many times, because our thinking is wrong.

It brings about separation. There is a lack of communication. This season of change don't mean that we are doing wrong, but we are leaving because of the marriage vows; to God, to serve.

The word of God lets us know that he that taketh a wife is to leave his mother's house and cleave to his wife. And the two shall become one. Gen. 2:24

For this cause, many leave a ministry. Of course, we love those in that ministry. We have developed a relationship, we've found new friends, it has become our church family.

VITAMINS OF HOPE

But God has said that we're to leave our mother's house and cleave to your wife. In this instant, we're leaving the one ministry to marry another. It doesn't mean that we no longer love our church family. But because of LOVE, we leave and become one to the Marriage of the ministry family.

For you see, it's because of LOVE, that we must move in with our husbands and wives. What the Lord is saying is, move in with your husband, for I've joined you to your husbandman, the ministry. For as a father loves a son, and a son honors his father in his service to others, so you must serve your husband. For I have indeed ordained this union; For my glory shall rein. The two shall become one, then how? Shall there then be division among my people? For this is the marriage that I've given my consent to. So then when ye come together as one, there shall be no division but unity in this house, in this family. For what cause is it that my children continued to fight among themselves. How then do this for my glory? But in selfishness and vain, there is no glory. I praise ye not: For there is only one body, but many members. One hand cannot fight against the other. Neither can one eye against the other. Nor one leg walk without the other. But it Is **only** when they become one in function that the mission is accomplished. One body but many members.

PAMELA FIELDS

For this is my word, and so shall it rein. Obey you children your Father. For this is my will concerning you. Because you are to LOVE one another as I've LOVED you. For this is my commandment. For this cause a house divided against itself cannot stand.

Today as we take the time to stop and listen, let's not only listen but obey. For then faith cometh by hearing, and hearing by the word of God! Have you heard since you believe?

By Angelina Cooks

16 | SQUEEZE IT OUT

God, your music does to me what
    Matches does when united with gas.

When you strike it there
    Is an explosion.

And after the explosion
    In my soul has started, the quench.

Nothing can quench my soul
    Except a dive into your anointing.

And after I dive into your anointing
    My spirit reacts like a sponge.

A big sponge that absorbs as much
    As I can until I'm drench and heavy.

PAMELA FIELDS

Then my soul says "yes" to your will
    As it squeezes back out on every one, I meet.
        And on every situation, I encounter.

I'll squeeze out until the next time
    When I can soak up some more.

17 | THE BREATH OF LIFE

Has God given you breath today?

Have you given your breath back to Him?

For the word of God declares:
Let everything that have breath,
Praise the Lord.

There is a day coming,
No longer will we breathe in the beauty of life.
We would have shut our eyes to the earth's glory.

The formation of clouds scattered
In a deep blue hue.

Big oaks and wee little daffodils

A garden of roses,
Red, white, pink, and yellow roses.

Boundless sea stretched far and wide.

Yes, the day is coming when
No longer we breathe in the beauty of life.
We would have shut our eyes to the earth's glory.

PAMELA FIELDS

The color of an orange,
Its juices are vital, men see.

The lights that rule by day,
The waking hour of the sun
Until it's going down.

And those to rule by night,
The moon and it's glow
And all the stars twinkle.

The hummingbird sings
And the blue jay and cardinal
Boast its colors bright.

People of color, of other lands,
Culture, customs and languages.

How best we can
Love our neighbor
Love our brother
Across this good ole land.

Give it back
This life.

Give it back
This beauty.

Give it back
This land in which we live.

Give it back to God
The breath you breathe
Give it back in praise.

Because a day is coming.

18 | CROSSROADS OF LIFE

At the crossroads of Life
The intercession of
Good and Bad.

One would cross the
Road toward Good
If they knew what lies ahead.

A road so strait
And narrow, only a few
Have found and chosen.

But all so many the boarder
Street they've chosen.
A street of glitter
And any imaginable party,
You'll find it there.

However, the way to destruction
The inner-city life
Has led many to drinking strong drink,
Lying, cursing, killing and stealing.
Too deep down this street
To ever find your way back.

But all too often
A stranger in the street,
He'll show you the path,
All you have to do is
Turn Around.

19 | A DIFFERENT KIND OF TREE

In the clutches of my heart
    A little seed is growing.

I'm chopping down the tree
    Where the other seed grew.

The growth of a seed requires nourishment,
    To feed this seed, I'll need love and lots of prayer.

I'm pulling up roots,
    Where once grew a different kind of tree.

Good habits, the fertilizer rich.
    The roots of this seed must be strong.

Breaking up the fallow ground
    Won't be easy.

The breaking through of the first blade
    Requires focused prayer.

But first I must remove
    This tree of dirty habits.
    This tree of damage to my body.
    This tree of lust and the tree of cheating.
    This tree of gossip
    This tree of lying.
    This tree of unforgiveness.

VITAMINS OF HOPE

I have to clean it all up
        Because it all must go.

So that my little seed of righteousness
        Will have room to stretch its branches.

Feed that spirit, that seed
        With the Love of Christ.

And watch it grow
        And grow and grow.

20 | RENEWED WINGS

Renewed wings of strength

To carry me a little

Further.

Replace the worn

And tattered wings

Of a bruised and

Battered soul.

21 | AN IMPORTANT MAN

An important man is not
Just a father
Nor just a husband

An important man is
A role model
Respected and admired

It makes a difference to him
Where he stands
And what he speaks

Society is represented by you
Your presence makes a difference
In their existence

Many could see that in your natural role
If you were where you should be in life
That it would strengthen the younger men coming under you

Who would look to you
And seek guidance to do better
That right there is why

You are such an important man.

22 | MENDING BURDENS

My load was overburdened.

My heart was heavy.

And my grief had overshadowed me.

My trails were awesome.

My words were few.

And my vision was blurred.

The winds of adversity were blowing.

Which opened up a channel releasing a flood of tears.

I refused to be comforted.

My smile took a vacation.

And my joy leaped a page.

Heartbroken as I was

Only the strong hands of God could mend.

23 | QUICKSAND

In the war of life
    The battles are fought
        And the battle ground is at sea.

And oh, how the bombs did explode.

Into the waters I plunged.
    Wet with the spirit
        And the will to survive.

Strokes upon strokes
    Until I reached the sandy shore.
        Only to find quicksand.

Save me, Oh God;
    For the waters
        Are come in unto my soul.

24 | SCATTER THE SEEDS

Scatter the seeds which I have given you. From the fruits of the spirit will you scatter.

Then I am going to irrigate the land with my presence.

Scatter the seeds, planting them one by one. But far many other ways will they be scattered.

As my presence invades the winds, I will blow them across the seasons of time.

Scattered the seeds through each fruit. Scattered branches stretched far and wide. Let them grow from your heart.

On soil rich and fertile, scatter the seeds. Then my presence will thunder down rain and wash away all impurities.

Let them dive off you onto others. Implant the seeds of righteousness through precept and example.

Then I will turn on the faucet of everlasting water to irrigate the land with my presence.

25 | IN THE NAME OF JESUS...

Have you ever woke up at the break of day and dreaded its coming because of some foreseen doom, but got up and faced it anyhow in the name of Jesus?

Has the routine of work and paying bills ever seemed like one endless cycle only to find you deeper and deeper in debt, but you continued the cycle anyhow in the name of Jesus?

Has winter after winter and the lack of a coat, shoes, boots, or some lack caused you to face the dark and cold winter day unprepared, but you faced each day despite being cold in the name of Jesus?

Have you ever missed a bus and had to wait for what seemed endlessly and patiently on another? And while you waited, anticipation of owning a car overwhelmed you. Even through it was cold or you were running late for an appointment, yet you waited anyhow in the name of Jesus?

Have you ever gone to a grocery store and because of the need began to pile things into the cart? Only because you were at the store and realized you were out of certain needed items, purchased these items, only to have to carry them home yourself, but carried them anyhow in the name of Jesus?

PAMELA FIELDS

Despite the hardship we find ourselves faced with on any given day. Despite this tangled up mess in which we live or have found our lives, one must remember, we are the children of a King, adopted in the Royal Family of our Lord and Savior Jesus. When we started this journey at the hour of our birth, it was already fore known that our destination would find us in the King's court. Like a puzzle that you've worked over and over again, the pieces of this puzzle are at hand. The pieces are disassembled and shaken up only to be placed back into place in the name of Jesus.

VITAMINS OF HOPE
Vitaminas de la Esperanza
INTERMISSION

26 | SUCCESSFUL...

This is a day when anything that you set out to do...
   You may become successful at it.

If you set out to have sex...
   You may become successful in making a baby.

If you set out to smoke drugs...
   You may become successful in becoming an addict.

If you set out to be blessed...
   The Lord said that
   He will bless your good works.
   And you will have good success.

27 | HAVE YOU EVER...

Have you ever taken the time to wonder how the sky looks totally different at night and why you can't see the stars in the day?

Have you ever wondered why bees only come out in summer and snow only falls in winter and why trees change colors in autumn?

Have you ever wondered why people paint their houses the color they paint them? And why construction workers always work on streets that don't need it?

Have you ever wondered why buses look different when they're full then when they are empty, and why children believe in Santa Claus?

Have you ever wondered about tomorrow and why what you do today will in some way determine the unforeseen destiny of all our tomorrows?

By Nikia Fields

28 | THE ENLIST

Already, God has got
Angels dropping out of
Airplanes from the sky for us.

They should already
Be here among us.

In order to join God's Army
You've got to enlist.

Special combat Angels
Are awaiting to be
Assigned to you.

But you've got to enlist first.
That's the way the rules go
Says the Commander and Chief.

So that you can be trained
And ready to do battle.

29 | FAITH IN THE BAG

Heaven bound, one step at a time.
It's in the bag.

Knocking at the door of Heaven's gates.
It's in the bag.

A weary soldier, completing the job.

Longing to hear from the
Master's tableland,

Well done thou good.
And faithful servant.

30 | BUILDING A SOUL

Building up each other in
> God's most Holy Name.

God's character revealed in good looking
> Men and good-looking women.

Portraits of character demonstrated
> In deed and in good will toward men.

Drawing the lost, broken, bruise and poor
> Like the sheep that was lost and then found.

Embracing that soul with love
> Building them up reviving them until they are revived,
>> Calling them back from the dead like Lazarus.

Building a soul with the fruit
> Of God's love with patience.

Souls may be fragile
> So please, build them with care.

31 | A POOL OF TEARS

Which pool, which pool today?

The battle gets hard sometimes
    And not easily won.

Grief builds up
    Pain kicks in
        And tears open its flood doors.

Like chains interlocking
    One behind the other.
        A stream of tears pour.

Letting you know that
    You're hurt
    You're broken hearted
    You're bent spirited
    You're bruise and torn
    And you're burdened down.

VITAMINS OF HOPE

Wet chains screaming for freedom,
        Are released but far from freedom felt.

While the mind is sending
        Pain signals like explosives
                And missiles in the midst of wartime affairs.

The body's a war field
        An adventure still.

But what will make
        The war stop?

Windshields and wipers
        Doing little to ease the stream of tears.

Life's a big continual blur
        As the tears roll down your face and cheeks.

Which pool, which pool this time?

Everyone having his own pool to fill.
        Across a vast sea of time.

The width of some
        And the depth of others
                Are not always the same.

PAMELA FIELDS

The bitter sweet reality
    Bitter tears amongst
        Sweet tears of joy.

Are the thorns in the flesh
    Sufficient for God's grace.

32 | THE CHARACTER OF THE ROSE

The Rose and all its beauty
    Imperfect amongst all its thorns.

Every one adding up
    To that many imperfections.

The tightness of the bulb must yield
    And open up to reveal its beauty.

Displaying a very shy,
    Charming and innocent character trait

A Rose, amongst flowers
    Arouses in its aroma
        A sweet scent of smells

Yet amongst all the other flowers
    A Rose is plucked
        To display its beauty, then dies.

33
AT THE GRAVESITE

At the gravesite
Is where I've learned
To dig up the ground
And to bury my sin.

Armed with a shovel
I began to dig within
My own soul every
Evil thought from within.

And with the shovel
I would go after that thought
Digging it up quickly to bury
It deep within the grave.

Sin is pleasurable, but you
Can die in your pleasure
So get rid of your sin
Before your sin gets rid of you.

Sex is pleasurable
But AIDS will take you out.

Getting high on booze and dope
Is pleasurable, but many have OD'd.

VITAMINS OF HOPE

Smoking cigarettes a social habit, pleasurable
But cancer buries you with a slow death.

At the gravesite it was
Either me or the sin
So of the two of us
One had to go, why not sin?

34 | AMALIKITES

An enemy amongst all
The people

Inwardly they have horns
And they sharpen their teeth
To growl at you.

They tuck their horns in and
They'll meet you at church
Disguising themselves to look
Like you and me.

The devastation that they reek
Causing headline news
And many a voices wept
Until there is no more
Power to weep

Although they hide their horns
They're found in places
Where our feet should not meet
So many cross aside the street
When it's the power
Of Jesus in you
That they really need to meet.

They're not Black,
Nor are they White.
They're not Hispanic
Nor Chinese,
They're Amalikites
An enemy amongst all the people.

35 | COBWEBS

Cobwebs have grown
  Where minds were
    Once polished and poised.

Cobwebs, like the connecting
  Blood source from the brain
    To the parts of the body.

Intricate and delicate
  Cobwebs just sprung
    All over the place.

The mind is collecting dust
  And cobwebs because the
    Mind is not being used any more.

Where once man figured
  Out mathematics equations and read books
    Exercising and toning the brain muscles.

Now rely them on computers
  And calculators. Vain words
    And vanity, not even a vocabulary.

Dust and cobwebs in the
  Chambers of the heart, a cold, dark and
    Dusty place with many scars and broken places.

PAMELA FIELDS

Love don't live there any more
    Love sprouts and grow in a
        Warm and caring soul.

The man's soul needs to be dusted.
    The dullness needs a glow, and its
        Vital organs polished until there is a high gloss.

Like the dusty old lamp
    In a favorite fairy tale
        Shine the soul with the Holy Ghost.

To light the fire in that cold old heart
    And to will the mind where once
        There was none.

36 | THE SPIRITUAL RODEO

Mounting up and riding
On the spirit of God.

Galloping upon the
Spirit of my faith.

The bulls got horns
And the devil's got two.

Herding sinners in
Riding horseback.

Roping them in the spirit
To brand them with the mark of the
Holy Ghost.

Bronco riding the devil
Until he lets them go.

PAMELA FIELDS

Steer wrestling his imps
In the mist of a good time.

Public exhibitions, programs
And the test of skills and talents,

Big hats and
Social affairs of the West,

The round up at the old wild west show
Never will be the same
Since the Holy Ghost
Bronco busters came to town.

37 | THAT'S JOY

I asked my child if she knew
Who Joy was?

I could tell by the frown on
Her face

And the attitude that
Accompanied.

So I set out to give my interpretation:

When you can smile without
Any probable reason, but because
Smiling makes you feel good,
That's Joy.

When the glow in your eyes
And the dimples in your cheeks
Make themselves be known,
That's Joy.

When life has embraced you
And the terribles of yesterday
Are readily dismissed,
That's Joy.

38 | THE WRONG ROOM

Has there ever been a time in your life
When you've gotten yourself ready,
>   Put on your best clothes, and combed your hair
>   In preparation and anticipation on being on schedule?

But the meeting you were to attend
Or the class group you're to meet with
>   Has already met and dismissed or perhaps
>   The group is now convening on the opposite side of the building.

But what's worst is that there is absolutely nothing
You will be able to say in your defense to explain
>   That you made it to the meeting on time but
>   Ended up in the wrong room.

As you make your entry
All heads are distracted
>   From what is being presented
>   As you spy an empty seat across the room.

Well sometimes in life we end up in places
Where we know that we should not be
>   Maybe it's something about the way
>   The majority greets you or doesn't greet you.

VITAMINS OF HOPE

Maybe your level of maturity
Is a complete give away.
> Perhaps you end up in the men's locker room
> When you should be in the women's.

Or perhaps you wander
> Into the lady's washroom
>> When you meant to go to the men's.

Somehow this incident
Awaken you to the fact
> That you don't belong there.
> That transition can be a rude awakening.

So wake up, keep focus
> Notice that these incidents
>> Never happens when you're in a crowd.

This is intended for individual growth
But the enemy wants to discredit you
> And send in spirits of discouragement,
>> Self-doubt, low self-esteem and confusion.

If he can do this
He has accomplished
> That which he set out to do
> So, wake up, keep focus and grow.

39 | DRINKING THE FLUIDS OF LOVE

Drinking Love is a vitamin

To men's soul.

Pour up a bottle of it

And drink it on down.

One hundred percent pure

Not imitation.

Not concentrate frozen

Just pure fluid, fresh all the time.

40 | UNUTTERED COMMUNICATION

Heaven is where I want to meet you,
On Holy Ground.

Tears of joy,
To match the smile on a glistening heart.

Heaven is where I want to meet you,
In Boundless Time.

Maturity's the key,
Understanding the slightest of all gestures.

Heaven is where I want to meet you,
When The Sun Goes Down.

Reading words of knowledge,
Written in the peak of wisdom.

Heaven is where I want to meet you,
When The Trumpet Sounds.

PAMELA FIELDS

Vision of hope,
A kindly display of unmeasured love.

Heaven is where I want to meet you,
With Every Pound.

Sun bright,
Stretches far across the silent skies blue.
Rolling clouds scattered.

Heaven is where I want to meet you,
Higher On Every Round.

Prayer wheel turning in the soul,
In a misty day, meditate I day and night.

Heaven is where I want to meet you,
Cause I'm Heaven Bound.

Nature's beauty glimpses,
Breaths of the breezes strong and calm.

Heaven is where I want to meet you,
Round And Round.

Twilight twinkling,
The desire of the wanting heart.

VITAMINS OF HOPE

Heaven is where I want to meet you,
That Great Town in The Sky.

Peace's perfect presence,
Presses and pierces with shimmering strength.

Heaven is where I want to meet you,
Where Mercy Is Found.

These are the prayers, unuttered
Vaporated off the tables of my heart.

Forming clouds of glory
That gathers with density toward a mighty time.

The seeds of a great harvest
Awaits rain as it pour down the
Blessings from answered prayers.

Closed eyes and tightly clasped hands
On bended knees in my secret place
Are uttered and unuttered communication
In prayers, lifted up toward heaven.

All other times
Are unuttered communication.

41 | COMING IN FROM THE STROM

It was plain for all to see,
From the trail of mud tracks
From whence the stranger came.

The stranger wasn't from these parts.
He looked different from us, he dressed different
And when he opened his mouth to speak, he talked
Differently too.

There was a distant glare in his eyes, a frozen glaze.
A Tear rolled down his face and as it did he smiled.
A very warm and tender smile of relief was shared.

He limped as he walked. His clothes worn and torn.
It was plain to see from the bruises and outer scars,
That it must have been quite a fight.

VITAMINS OF HOPE

His testimony he shared
Talked of such an attack:

Revealing a past of a tremendous amount of wealth and material gain. A man of great luxury. The man talked of how he had it all. "The best that money could buy, a loving family, supportive and dear. Who would have though that I would lose it all?" he said sadly as he continued. "Happiness was at its mountain peak. No one, no, no one had it so complete."

I thought about the man of riches, Job. The rich man in Biblical times of the land of Uz. Perfect and upright before God. Blessed to have had ten children. Job lost it all, his wealth, and his family. And then sickness came to add to his pain of grief and sorrow.

I then thought about the man of wealth, Jesus. A King of Kings, Jesus had it all in Gloryland. Many mansions, a street paved with gold, angels who attended to his every need. Jesus gave it all up to be born in a stable. Born to be the son of a carpenter. Then engaged in his ministry with not even a place to lay His head. Tempted of the devil forty days and forty nights, no food did He eat. Betrayed, scorned, spat on, whipped and bruised. One word to the father in heaven and the angels would have been immediately dispatched to come to his aid. The hammer wedged nails into his hands and feet. Then He was lifted up on a stake to die. The blood poured from his body in every imaginable place, then they pierced Him in his side.

PAMELA FIELDS

As I listened to the man's testimony, I could see right off that the man was a special vessel which God had prepared for a specific purpose.

Somehow, I knew him. Beneath the ungroomed build up of facial hair; the dirty and ragged clothes he wore, stained from days upon days of many wears; beneath the heavy mud-covered boots, missing tooth and decaying others and the many other wounds in which this man carried; I knew him. I knew his history and I knew his future. I knew that nothing will ever again hurt him.

The man pulled up a chair and sat down. He welcomed the caring and the warmth in which he was experiencing. There was peace as everyone at the little church greeted the stranger with love.

Somehow, I knew that the man had came in to visit our church to get out of the storm. I knew that we would never again see him on this side of heaven.

42 | WHERE IS THE GOOD TEACHERS' GRAVEYARD?

THERE MUST BE A GOOD TEACHERS' GRAVEYARD. A deposit somewhere just building up of the positive character of teachers of old. I'm talking about teachers born to educate. Teachers who knew how to pique the interest of the youth of our society. When we were minus all the extra programs. And the classroom consisted of the students and that teacher. Her in-depth knowledge of reading, writing and arithmetic, social studies and science. A time when the only instruments used were a blackboard, chalk, a point stick, books and of course her desk where an apple so graciously sat.

These teachers worked long dedicated hours, but were gifted in imparting knowledge into the minds of youth in that day. There is no apple sitting on the desk of teachers today. In the halls of schools across the nation, an echo breathes, a weak cry, whispering of what makes up a real teacher. For surely the

PAMELA FIELDS

technology of today in the hands of a real teacher should win a better grade. This is a day when the teachers should be tested, not academically, but profoundly. For today, they are acclaimed this and proclaimed that. What was once a dedication, is now just a job. The driving factor, how much money, moving up the latter to administration, or it's a career. They are an elite group, but the imprint of their predecessors are blowing in the winds tossed, and turned. Where are the real teachers' grave? Where is the depository? The cry may be weak, but the pulse still beats.

In a troubled world, we are losing so many of promise. The potential of these we lose is like a stain against the profession. Smeared in the gutter of time and wasted. Their opportunity may never come again. Teaching is a skill which gives us an opportunity to impart good. Reaching the mind in an effort to mode and fertilize it to grow until individuality sprouts and independence takes over and maturity develops.

43 | SLAVE

My wrist:
    Like a beauty mark
    I wear an identification bracelet.
    Wear I, for all to see.
    In the presence of all without shame.
    I lift my arms and boast who's I am.

My neck:
    A permanent collar of gold.
    Like a branding iron,
    Never to be removed.
    No thief by day.
    Nor robber by night could ever take.

My tears:
    Were real, every one.
    Bitter tears wiped away by my Master,
    Each with sweet rewards.
    Sweet tears of joy.
    Real, every one.

The purchase:
    A price paid with blood.
    A sacrifice of blood and
    An open display of love.
    The price of my soul
    Would never have been redeemed,
    Had my Master not come for me.

PAMELA FIELDS

The purpose:
    My Master choose me to be a leader.
    Like a torch does He lead me.
    Warm unto my soul,
    And visible unto my sight.
    Am I to lead others the way?

His presence:
    In the beauty of Holiness, I come.
    Preparing always to come before His presence.
    Nothing but praise,
    In dance and thanks to my Master.
    I render with uplifted hands,
    And hallelujahs.

44 | SPICES

People are like spices.
    Some are strong in flavor.
Some weak, some hot,
    And some very distinctive in taste.

The spices are a people
    That bare the burden
But the meat gets
    All the credit.

Strong in taste and flavor,
    It gets the work done.
Selective spices each
    Having its own flavor.

Bland flavor is what meat
    Is without spices.

PAMELA FIELDS

Like a game of Monopoly
    It's no fun unless some one lands on your property,
No fun when everyone is conserving funds,
    And no one is buying property.

Spices makes things happen
    Spices are interesting tidbits in life.
Salt without flavor is no good,
    And bland flavors are such a bore.

45 | THE BLIND MAN

Too many years have gone by
    The man just closed his eyes
        One day and refused to open and see.

The blind man had someone to
    Call me, it was no other that he
        Wanted in his time of need.

So diligent was I in answering
    The call. I vowed to keep
        Him in his time of sickness.

So many bad habits he refused to correct.
    So many lost lessons he refused to learn.
        Helpless as I was, he refused to pray.

Many others I see as I travel to and from.
    Cane in hand, they seem to have learned their way.
        A book of Braille, a guide dog to protect.

The way I understand, there is more than
    One way. Open up your eyes Mr. Blind Man
        Or figure out how to pray your way.

PAMELA FIELDS

So many years, the blind man
    Only see the void and destruction
        Of his own thoughts, void of understanding.

What lies behind your dreams
    Mr. Blind Man? What lies behind your
        Rosy pictures? Your faith without works?

Open up your eyes and see
    Another way. Open up your eyes
        And hear the truth.

Open up and see. Feel the answer
    In a touch. Understanding a real
        Language, deeper than words.

Know that on the other side of your doubts, lie the answer.
    On the other side of your fears, there is truth.
        On the other side of darkness is light.

Break through the barriers of
    These images which blind you.
        Tear them all down.

A false hope have I've been
    Steering and guiding, leading
        And pushing. A false persuasion.

Cause after all the persuasion
    Is done and over, you still
        Claim to be blind.

VITAMINS OF HOPE

Sometimes I think it easier to
    Help some other blind person
        But my vow, I've given you.

Can you at least peek to see
    My enormous task? The task, meaning
        Assignment or job, a chore, or responsibility.

The task's will is not done
    Til you see, or die.
        And then will my labor be in vain?

So in this desperate time
    And hopeless hour, I have no other choice
        Than to report to the task giver.

Dear Father in Haven:

The assignment I vowed to you
    To hold the hand of and to keep
        From falling during this time of sickness I kept.

But this one thing you know to be true
    My vow to you is deeper and pure.
        The prayer that blind eyes be opened, I believe.

So because this problem is tougher than
    Any math problem I've ever encountered
        I'm giving this one to you.

PAMELA FIELDS

**I'm letting go of his hand,
But not my vow. Let him fall if you will
But don't let him get up without seeing.**

46 | SPIRIT OF STRUGGLE

The roles of our forefathers
So much ponder I
Their cries of pain and lack
Etch way back.

In a day where the land
Flows with milk and honey
Education is for all the people
And it's not the hand-me-downs
To determine a man's table.

The history of our people
Leads and guides us like a beacon light
So much knowledge to glean
From their struggle and strength.

Surely my pains in life
Is nothing by comparison
Yet my endurance
Must be just as great.

Their fight for freedom
A common thread which yoked them in unity

PAMELA FIELDS

Fights for rights, equality and justice
Must continue to be the aim.

With every water fountain
That I drink from
And every public school that I enter
The spirit of struggle has already been.

A spirit which cries from the grave
Of every soul whose blood was shed for the cause
Cries who suffered for the treasures which
Many today have abandoned or
Taken for granted.

Souls who scream out from the grave
That longed for freedom, and never found till death's last
Screams at the many who entangle themselves
In bondage with the pollutants of task makers
Without whips.

Rivers upon rivers of tears
Which have long since dried
But the memory haunts
Of the ghostly past.

Memories of how it must have been
Override the memories of how it should have been
Hanging on to the patches and piecework
Of an intricate history.

Until another piece
Can be sewn together

VITAMINS OF HOPE

Into the overall picture
Of how it really was.

The accomplishments
Of an unprivileged people
Who managed delicacies
Out of discarded pig foot and chitterlings.

A people who
Became poets, scientists, and inventors
Lacking proper education
Taught themselves to read.

A people who were introduced to the Bible
By the White masters and slave owners
But the Black man showed his
White brother how to live the Bible.

How can I cry today
When their pain has paved my way?

In my pockets are treads and bits of lent
But my memories so rich
By the many adventures
Which led to my victory.

Enriched by a people
Who fought for me
Beautifully carved in my memory
A delicate piece of fine art.

PAMELA FIELDS

Molded into my impression
So life like as the spirits of struggle reveal themselves
Every character, every role and every script
A detailed work of artistry.
Bravo, bravo, I applaud thee.

47 | THAT UNEXPLAINABLE FEELING

It's called renewed strength.
It's called abundant joy.
It's called unmerited favor.
It's called divine love.
It's called being chosen,
Hand picked,
Broken
Then put back together,
And molded,
By The Potter's Hand.

Plucked like a flower,
For the unique purpose
That it serves,
With its beauty,
And with its sweet scent.

To understand that purpose
Is to understand
Who you are.
You're a child of God
Born for a purpose.

48 | ANGELS AT THE DOOR

As I laid my head,
I prayed to the Lord
My soul to keep.

As my listless body laid in a state of unconsciousness through the night, unable to defend the attacks of evil spirits that creep during the night. The angels stood guard at the door of my life.

My eyes are still very heavy,
With sleep as I am aroused by
The angels as they knock at the door.

Angels are at the door
They are at the dawn of a brand-new day.
As they call my name into conscience, my sleepy eyes wake.

Praise the Lord,
And thank you,
For this another day.

49 | A LAWYER IN THE COURTROOM

There was a charge against me
    As a saint of God.

It came from one who was
    So dear to my heart.

An attack of the devil
    I didn't see it coming.

Satan came in and
    He stole my child.

Planted a seed of bitterness
    And created a lie.

The judge was on the bench
    And the trial date was set.

The accusation was made
    It was time to confess.

I wasn't guilty of the charge
    And I knew that for sure.

Many times, since my case
    I didn't understand, my life was on trail
    Because the devil wanted my head.

PAMELA FIELDS

I had to trust in God
>Through every tear to see me through.

So the States Attorney pointed right in my face,
>Accused me of abuse.

He accused me of abandonment
>Me a drug addict and other lies too.

For nine days and nights
>I didn't know where my child was.

Never thought I would have to fight
>Just to prove my love.

My heart was so empty
>My life wasn't complete.

I had to fight the devil
>For my child to return home to me.

He wanted to pimp her before me
>But God said NO!

I'll save her, God said
>From drowning, just hold on and don't let go.

We went to court
>No dry eye was found.

I stood on my faith
>And everything that wasn't like God
>Had to come down.

>By: Angelina Beck

50 | THE PROCEDURE

Who am I? What must I be?
I never thought at age twenty, this would be me.

Living in a facility owned by the state.
Getting fed three times a day.

Losing much weight
I remembered; I was a civilian living free.

But one day the FBI
Came and snatched me.

They took me to this place called
Cook County Department of Correction.

Where I sat in a bullpen
(I imagined) about a week.

I guess it was all in my mind
That's the way it felt to me.

PAMELA FIELDS

Going through some procedure
Called coughing and squatting.

Oh! What was that for?
Plenty of people still blow refer and rock smoke.

They issue us blue uniforms
Labeled D.O.C.

Letting you know
You're now their property.

Now you're finally through all that mess.
Getting the most hateful part off your chest.

Now you're headed for what they call the tier.
Where there are forty to fifty women yelling.

"On the new, they're here."
What is this? What must this be?

I've never been in such a big facility
Where there are so many women
Ranting, raving, screaming, yelling and misbehaving.

It was about 8:30 to 9:00 p.m.
The next thing I knew, an officer in a blue uniform
Opened up the door and said
"Clear the day room."

VITAMINS OF HOPE

I had these numbers written on my arm, 98 ----
I didn't know what they were for.

Oh! 98 must be the year
As I said sadly crying out tears.

Then some girl yelled at me
Take a shower my dear, you see.

I was confused and didn't know what to do
Hopping into a cold shower frozen through and through.

After I came out, rest was assured.
Some girl named "Lil baby" said
Do you know your room?

I said room five I think
Oh! D--- you're in the room with bull dagging Janie.

I was afraid but headed to lay down.
Bull dagging Janie didn't make a sound.

Someone was screaming, breakfast ladies
I just turned over yarning feeling hazy.

The next thing I knew someone was yelling
Board of Education ladies.

PAMELA FIELDS

I thought I was goin crazy
Time to learn the facts, you don't know the rules.

Everybody on P1 must go to school
Who am I? What must this be?

Come to find out someone paid my bond
The officer said, pack, yo! You're going home.

It was my mother awaiting
For her beautiful daughter.

Smiling and grinning as happy as could be
As her child walked out D.O.C.

> This is what every inmate must go through
> I'm a living witness. People, please spare
> Yourselves of this place.

> **Signed, Anonomus**
> **98 ----**

VITAMINS OF HOPE

ACKNOWLEDGMENTS

First and foremost, I'd like to thank God for allowing me to go through my journey of life in which I have been able to learn and grow from my circumstances, and change my challenges into this beautiful work of art and book series of poems.

And to my mother, Leola Reynolds, whom told the best stories when I was growing up. My love for her and her stories as she told us as we were growing up were quite splendid.

And to my readers, I am grateful for your support I'd like to offer some wisdom. When an older person has a story to tell, sit down and listen because it will be a good story, one of true wisdom.

ABOUT THE AUTHOR

Born to Gentle Frank Fields and Leola Reynolds, Pamela Fields grew up on the south side of Chicago, Illinois, where she attended several elementary schools and Wendell Phillips High School, all schools located in Chicago, Illinois. She also attended Harold Washington Junior College and would go on to major is Early Childhood Education. She later attended Prestige Nurse Aide Training Academy, where she attained her certification as a CNA. Both of the selected majors were encouraged by her experiences of not wanting any child to be left behind, nor any older adult left uncared for.

Fields held the position of being the oldest of her siblings, one sister, and two brothers. She refers to her brothers and sister as stair-steps as each sibling is one year apart from the other. Fields acknowledge her siblings and Richard Reynolds, her superhero and second husband to her mother, for preparing her to understand and learn several tactics of dealing with the way of the world. Fields has three children: Nikia Fields, Edward Fields, and Shana Edwards, and she loves them all dearly. Her children have blessed her with eight grandchildren, and Fields continues to shower them with the educational packages from her homemade learning lessons.

PAMELA FIELDS

Getting into the professional side of life, Fields was employed at several early learning centers. She also worked as a CNA on weekends, and she spent a few evening hours taking care of her mother. Her years of employment with others have led her to her Happily Ever After, becoming a future best-selling author with S.H.E. PUBLISHING LLC, and starting up two businesses simul- taneously, one being K.I.N.D.N.E.S.S. Kare (*Keys IN Developing & Navigating Effective Social Solutions*), a childcare service, and Pam's Baking Handz.

Ultimately, Fields purpose and passion is to bring together ordinary people like you and me with the commitment to encourage us to love one another. She believes that it's the small efforts of a friendly smile, the gift of gratitude, praying for one another, and small acts of kindness that will change the world one day, one hour, and one second at a time. It only takes a second to yield a smile and patience doesn't cost anything.

Thanks for reading!
Please add a short review on
Amazon and S.H.E. PUBLISHING LLC.
Let me know your thoughts!